Sunny-Side Up

*Good Morning Recipes
to Start Your Day*

Cindy Grubb

HARVEST HOUSE PUBLISHERS
Eugene, Oregon 97402

Library of Congress Catalog-in-Publication Data

Grubb, Cindy
     Sunny-side up / Cindy Grubb.
           p. cm.
     ISBN 1-56507-593-5
     1. Breakfasts. I. Title.
     TX733.G635   1997
     641.5'2-dc21   96-39084
                                          CIP

Design and production by Left Coast Design, Portland, Oregon

To

Mother and Daddy,

Ann and Frank Nolan,

who are up in heaven.

You taught me that with God,

all things are possible.

Without Him, this book never

would have happened.

All happiness
depends on a leisurely
breakfast.

Say good morning
with a warm meal
filled with good things
and sprinkled
with love.

Rise & Shine Breads and Muffins

Cheery Cranberry Bread

2 cups flour
1½ teaspoons baking powder
½ teaspoon baking soda
¼ cup butter or oil
1 teaspoon orange peel
¾ cup orange juice
1 egg, beaten
1 cup sugar
1 cup cranberries
½ cup chopped nuts

Sift flour, baking powder, and baking soda. Cut
in butter. Combine orange peel, orange juice, and
egg. Add sugar, then add to dry ingredients. Mix
to moisten. Fold in berries and nuts. Put in
greased loaf pan. Bake for 60 minutes at 350°.

Golden Bubble Ring

2 packages active dry yeast
½ cup warm water
½ cup milk, scalded
½ cup shortening
½ cup sugar
1 teaspoon salt

4 to 4 1/2 cups flour
2 eggs, beaten
melted butter
1 teaspoon cinnamon

Soften yeast in warm water. Combine milk, shortening, ½ cup sugar and salt. Cool to lukewarm. Add 1 cup flour; beat well. Add yeast mixture and eggs. Beat smooth. Mix in remaining flour or enough to make a soft dough. Knead on floured surface till smooth and elastic (8 to 10 minutes). Place in greased bowl, turning once to grease surface. Cover and let rest 10 minutes. Shape into about 28 golfball-size balls. Roll each in melted butter, then in sugar and cinnamon mixture. Arrange in well-greased 9-inch tube pan. Let double in size, 1 hour. Bake at 350° for 35 to 40 minutes. Cool in pan 15 to 20 minutes. Invert on rack; remove pan.

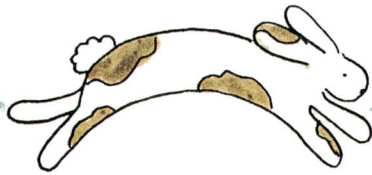

Carrot Pineapple Muffins

2 eggs
½ teaspoon salt
1 cup sugar
1 teaspoon cinnamon
1½ cups flour
2/3 cup oil
1 cup grated carrot
1 teaspoon vanilla
1 teaspoon baking powder
cup crushed pineapple, drained
1 teaspoon baking soda

Beat eggs and sugar together. Add remaining
ingredients and beat well. Fill greased muffin tins
three quarters full. Bake 25 minutes at 350°.
Makes 12 muffins.

Applesauce Puffs

2 cups Bisquick
½ cup sugar
1 teaspoon cinnamon
1 egg

¼ cup milk
1 cup applesauce
2 tablespoons oil

Topping
1 teaspoon cinnamon
melted butter

½ cup sugar

Combine first seven ingredients in a bowl. Stir vigorously for 30 seconds. Grease muffin pan or line with paper cups. Fill cups two-thirds full. Bake at 400° for 15 to 20 minutes. Cool slightly. Dip tops in melted butter and roll in cinnamon-sugar topping. Makes 12 large muffins.

Clever Coffee Cake

1 package yellow cake mix
1 package (small) butterscotch
   instant pudding
3/4 cup oil
3/4 cup water
1 teaspoon vanilla

1 teaspoon butter flavoring
4 eggs
1/2 cup chopped nuts
2 teaspoons cinnamon
1/4 cup sugar

Glaze
1 cup powdered sugar
3 tablespoons milk
2 teaspoons vanilla

Blend cake mix and pudding. Add oil, water, and flavorings, and mix. Add eggs one at a time. Mix at high speed for 8 minutes. In a small bowl, mix together cinnamon and sugar; set aside. Grease bundt pan. Spread one-third nuts on bottom, then layer one-third cake batter, and one-third cinnamon sugar. Repeat layers, ending with batter on top. Bake for 65 minutes at 350°. Cool for 8 minutes. Remove from pan and allow to cool before glazing. For the glaze, mix sugar, milk, and vanilla.

10

Grandma's Strawberry Bread

2 cups sugar
3 cups flour
1 teaspoon cinnamon
1 teaspoon baking soda
½ teaspoon salt
2 cups frozen strawberries, thawed
1 cup pecans
4 eggs
1¼ cup cooking oil

Mix all ingredients together in mixing bowl. Grease and
flour three 8x4x2-inch loaf pans. Bake
1 hour at 350°. A variation: Increase cinnamon to
1 tablespoon and nuts to 1¼ cups. These freeze nicely
so you can bake ahead.

Lumberjack Loaf

2 loaves frozen bread dough
1 pound sausage
garlic powder
8 ounces mozzarella cheese, grated
¼ cup Romano cheese
4 eggs

Let bread rise; pat out on two cookie sheets. Brown sausage with garlic powder; mix browned sausage with cheeses. Beat eggs and add to sausage mixture. Spread on half bread dough; turn other half over it and bake according to bread package directions. Makes 2 loaves. One loaf can be frozen after baking.

Your own soul is nourished
when you are kind.
Proverbs

Geraldine's Drop Biscuits

1½ cups Flour
½ teaspoon salt
¼ tablespoon baking soda
1 tablespoon baking powder
1 cup buttermilk

Sift Flour; add salt, baking soda, and baking
powder into a bowl, then add buttermilk. Mix well.
Drop onto greased pan. Makes 8 biscuits. Bake in 400°
oven until done, about 20 minutes. Split open, add
butter and jam, and enjoy!

Just Banana Bread

½ cup butter or margarine
1 cup sugar
2 eggs
2 cups sifted flour
½ teaspoon salt
1 teaspoon baking soda
3 large bananas, mashed
1 cup nuts

Cream butter and sugar together. Beat in eggs, one at a time. Sift remaining dry ingredients and add to mixture. Beat in mashed bananas. Add nuts. Pour into greased loaf pan. Bake at 350° for 50 to 60 minutes, or when inserted toothpick pulls out clean.

Muffin Surprise

1 egg
¾ cup milk
1 cup raisins
1 chopped apple
½ cup oil
1 cup flour
⅓ cup quick oats

⅓ cup sugar
3 teaspoons baking
   powder
1 teaspoon salt
1 teaspoon nutmeg
2 teaspoons cinnamon

Beat egg. Stir in remaining ingredients, mixing just to moisten. Pour into 12 greased muffin cups until three-fourths full. Bake at 400° for 15 to 20 minutes. Serve cool or piping hot with butter. Makes 12 muffins.

Aunt Jo's Coffee Cake

Batter
2 cups sugar
1 cup butter
4 eggs
3½ cups flour
3 teaspons baking powder
1 cup milk

Filling
1 cup sugar
3 teaspoons cinnamon
½ cup chopped nuts

Preheat oven to 350°. Cream 2 cups sugar, butter, and eggs, beating after each egg. Sift flour and baking powder, then add in alternately with milk. Mix 1 cup sugar, cinnamon, and chopped nuts for filling. Pour one-quarter batter in angel food cake pan, then one-quarter filling. Repeat three more times, ending with filling. Bake for 70 minutes. Remove from pan and drizzle with frosting.

Frosting
Add small amounts of milk to 2 cups sifted confectioners' sugar for drizzling consistency. Add dash salt and 1 teaspoon vanilla. Drizzle over cake and allow to drip down the sides.

Mom's Cinnamon Rolls

1 cup shortening
¾ cup sugar
2 teaspoons salt
1 cup boiling water
2 packages yeast

7½ cups flour
1 cup cold water
4 eggs, beaten
butter
sugar and cinnamon

Frosting

2 cups powdered sugar
dash salt

1 teaspoon vanilla
add milk to desired consistency

Cream first 4 ingredients. Soften yeast in water. Add flour, water, and eggs. Dough mixture will be sticky and soft. Divide into 4 equal parts and place in 4 bowls. Cover with wet towel and refrigerate overnight. Turn out (1 bowl at a time) on floured surface and roll out into rectangle. Spread with butter and sprinkle generously with sugar and cinnamon mixture. Roll up and mesh ends with palms. Do next 3 dough piles. Cut each roll into 10 equal parts. Place in two greased (bottom and sides) 9 x 13-inch pans (4 rows of 4) and one large loaf pan. Let rise until double in size. Bake for 20 minutes at 350°. Let cool 5 minutes. Loosen sides with knife and turn out on counter. Cool, cut apart, and frost.

Orange Breakfast Ring

¾ cup sugar
3 tablespoons grated orange peel
2 packages (of 10) or 3 packages (of 6)
   buttermilk biscuits
⅓ cup butter, melted
1 three-ounce package cream cheese
½ cup powdered sugar
2 tablespoons orange juice

Grease a bundt pan. Combine sugar and orange peel.
Dip biscuits in melted butter and roll in sugar-
orange peel mixture. Place on side in bundt pan.
Bake 20 minutes at 350°. Combine cream cheese
and powdered sugar. Add orange juice and beat.
Drizzle over hot biscuits.

Nutty Apple Bread

2 cups chopped
  apples (generous)
1 cup sugar
1 stick margarine
1 egg
1 ½ cups flour
1 teaspoon baking soda

1 teaspoon cinnamon
½ teaspoon salt
½ teaspoon allspice
½ teaspoon cloves
½ cup pecans, chopped
½ cup raisins

Place apples and sugar in a medium mixing bowl; let stand for 10 to 15 minutes. Melt margarine and pour over apples; beat egg and mix with apple mixture. Add dry ingredients, pecans, and raisins. Pour into 2 greased loaf pans and bake approximately 25 minutes at 350°. Test with toothpick.

Eggnog Holiday Bread

3 cups flour, sifted
¾ cup sugar
1 tablespoon
  baking powder
1 teaspoon salt
½ teaspoon nutmeg

1½ cups dairy eggnog
1 egg, beaten
¼ cup butter, melted
¾ cup chopped pecans
¾ cup candied fruit

In a large bowl sift together flour, sugar, baking powder, salt, and nutmeg. In a separate bowl mix eggnog, egg, and butter. Add wet ingredients to dry, stirring well. Add pecans and fruit. Bake in greased loaf pan at 350° for 60 to 70 minutes.
Cool on a wire rack. Delicious with cheese and cold cuts.

Make Hay While the Sun Shines Pancakes & Waffles

If you shout a pleasant greeting to a friend too early in the morning, it will be taken as a curse.

Proverbs

Grandpa Seidel's Famous Pancakes

3 eggs
1½ cups sour cream
1½ cups buttermilk
1½ cups cake flour
1 teaspoon baking soda
2 tablespoons sugar
1 teaspoon salt
2 ounces Mazola oil
maple syrup
powdered sugar

In large mixing bowl beat eggs well. Add sour cream and buttermilk, mix well. Sift dry ingredients twice in separate bowl. Add to sour cream/buttermilk mixture. Beat 2 minutes. Add oil and stir well (add more flour if you want thicker pancakes). Cook on hot griddle and serve with maple syrup and powdered sugar.

23

Gingerbread Waffles

½ cup butter or margarine
½ cup (firmly packed)
   dark brown sugar
½ cup light molasses
2 eggs, separated
1 cup milk
2 cups all-purpose flour
1½ teaspoons
   baking powder

1 teaspoon cinnamon
1 teaspoon ground ginger
¼ teaspoon ground cloves
¼ teaspoon salt
lightly sweetened
   whipped cream
applesauce

Cream together the butter and brown sugar. Beat in the molasses, egg yolks, and milk. Sift flour, baking powder, cinnamon, ground ginger, ground cloves, and salt together. Beat egg whites until soft peaks form. Stir dry ingredients into creamed mixture, then fold in egg whites. Pour batter into preheated waffle iron and bake until lightly browned. Makes four 6 x 10 ½-inch waffles. Serve with lightly sweetened whipped cream and applesauce.

24

German Pancakes

This pancake puffs over the pan. It has a soft inside and is brown and crusty on the outside.

4 eggs
⅔ cup flour
1 teaspoon salt

⅔ cup milk
3 tablespoons butter
powdered sugar

Butter a heavy 10-inch ovenproof skillet. Preheat oven to 450°. Beat the eggs with a fork. Slowly add flour, beating continually. Stir in salt and milk. Pour the batter into the skillet and drop the butter by teaspoonfuls into the batter, spreading evenly. Bake at 450° for 15 minutes. Reduce heat to 350° and bake another 10 minutes. Remove from oven and sift powdered sugar over the top. Serve with warm maple syrup or squeeze the juice from lemon wedges over it.

Apple Cinnamon Pancakes

6 tablespoons butter
2 large apples, peeled, cored,
  and sliced (McIntosh
  apples work well)
3 tablespoons lemon juice
1/4 teaspoon ground cinnamon
5 tablespoons powdered sugar

3 eggs at room temperature
1/4 teaspoon salt
1/2 cup all-purpose flour
1/2 cup lowfat milk
powdered sugar

Preheat oven to 425°.

Over medium heat, melt the butter in a 10-inch skillet or shallow pan; remove from heat. (If the skillet doesn't have an oven-proof handle, wrap it with several layers of foil.) Set aside two tablespoons melted butter in a medium bowl.

In a large bowl, mix apple slices with lemon juice. In a small bowl, stir cinnamon into sugar. Sprinkle the sugar mixture over the apple slices; toss to mix. Put the skillet back on the burner on medium heat. Add the apples and cook, stirring often, for 3 or 4 minutes, or until the slices are tender but still hold their shape. Remove from heat and spread apple slices evenly over the bottom of the skillet.

To the bowl (or a blender container or food processor) containing the reserved two tablespoons of butter—add the eggs, salt, flour, and milk. Beat this batter until smooth. Pour the batter over the apples. Bake about 20 minutes, or until pancake is golden and puffy. Invert immediately onto a warm platter so the apples are on top. Dust with powdered sugar and serve at once.

Barnyard Oven Pancakes

½ pound bacon (or salt pork)
3 eggs
1 quart milk
½ cup flour
2½ tablespoons sugar
¼ teaspoon salt
Pinch of pepper
butter
lingonberries or other berry sauce or syrup

Brown bacon in frying pan and drain off excess grease. Beat eggs, then add milk and dry ingredients. Pour over bacon, mixing slightly. Bake in 350° oven (still in frying pan) for one hour or until brown and well set. Serve hot from frying pan with butter, lingonberries, or other berry sauce or syrup.

27

Fear less -
hope more,
eat less -
chew more,
whine less -
breathe more,
talk less -
say more,
hate less -
love more,
and all good
things
will be yours.

· Swedish Proverb ·

28

Swedish Pancakes

2 cups flour
½ teaspoon baking powder
3 tablespoons sugar
½ teaspoon salt
4 eggs
2¾ cups milk

1 teaspoon vanilla
2 tablespoons butter or
    margarine, melted
lingonberries or other
    berry sauce or syrup
fruit for garnish

Mix dry ingredients in bowl and set aside. Mix wet ingredients in a larger bowl. Add dry ingredients to wet ingredients. Add butter and stir into mix. Mix ingredients with whisk, taking care not to overmix (small lumps are okay).

Spray shortening into a crepe pan (or large skillet) and heat. Add ½ cup mix; tilt pan until bottom and sides are coated with mix. Let cook, pushing back sides as they dry. Flip pancake when lightly browned and finish cooking. Make sure you don't overcook.

It's best to cook up a batch before serving (keeping them warm in oven). Serve with lingonberries or other berry sauce or syrup and butter. Garnish with other fruit for a festive breakfast dish.

Sunny Strawberry Pancakes

4 cups Bisquick
¼ teaspoon baking soda
2 cups milk
4 eggs
melted butter for griddle

¼ cup sugar
8 ounces cream cheese
7 ounces marshmallow
cream
frozen strawberries

Mix Bisquick baking soda, and milk. Separate eggs. Mix yolks into batter.

Ladle batter onto hot frying pan or griddle with melted butter. Cook until golden brown.

Beat egg whites until stiff, then add sugar. Mix with cream cheese and marshmallow cream, and put between pancakes. Joy with frozen strawberries.

Pecan & Rolled Oat Pancakes

¾ cup whole wheat flour
½ cup all-purpose flour
½ cup oats
¼ cup cornmeal
1 teaspoon baking powder
1 teaspoon baking soda
⅓ cup butter, cut into small pieces
2 eggs
2 cups buttermilk
¼ cup honey
½ cup chopped pecans
sprinkle of nutmeg

Combine and blend well all dry ingredients. Add butter pieces with fork and mix well. In another bowl, beat together eggs and buttermilk, then honey. Stir in flour mixture and mix well. Fold in the pecans.

Ladle batter onto hot frying pan or griddle with melted butter. Cook until golden brown. Serve with warm maple syrup or choice of topping. Serves 2-6*.

* 2 hungry men or 4 regular breakfast eaters or 6 dieters

Honey Butter

½ cup butter or margarine
¼ cup honey

Beat butter or margarine until creamy; gradually beat in honey. Great on biscuits, waffles, and pancakes!

Farm Fresh Egg Dishes

Be pleasant
until ten o'clock in
the morning,
and the rest of the
day will take care
of itself.

Train Wreck

½ pound bacon or ham
   (optional)
6 to 10 potatoes, diced
1 medium onion
   (optional)
1 small green pepper
   (optional)
1 pound sliced mushrooms
8 to 12 eggs

½ cup milk
salt and pepper to taste
2 cups cheese
salsa
sour cream
margarine (if needed for
   frying)

If using bacon, dice and fry it in a large skillet. Remove bacon
from grease and use the bacon grease to fry the potatoes, onion,
pepper, and mushrooms, stirring (to keep from burning) until
soft. Add eggs, milk, salt, and pepper. Mix all together and add
cheese. Cook until eggs are firm. Serve with salsa and sour cream.
If using ham instead of bacon, fry potatoes in margarine.

Best Breakfast Quiche

2 pounds yellow onions,
  chopped
3 tablespoons butter
1½ tablespoons flour
3 eggs
⅔ cup light cream
¾ cup Swiss cheese,
  grated

1 teaspoon salt
pepper
pinch of nutmeg
9-inch partially cooked
  pastry shell
4 slices bacon, cooked
  and then crumbled

In a heavy skillet, sauté the onions in butter over very low heat, stirring occasionally until onions are extremely tender and a golden yellow. Sprinkle with the flour, mix well, and continue to cook slowly for another three minutes. Remove from heat and allow to cool.

Whisk together the eggs and cream in a bowl. Blend in the salt, pepper, and nutmeg. Arrange the onions in the bottom of the pastry shell, then sprinkle with bacon pieces. Pour the egg mixture over the onions and sprinkle with cheese. Bake in the upper third of a preheated 375° oven for 25 to 30 minutes, or until the quiche has puffed and browned.

Buenos Dias Chili Casserole

4-seven ounce cans whole mild green chilies, drained
1 pound Monterey Jack cheese, cut into 1/4-inch slices
5 eggs, beaten
1 cup milk
1/4 cup flour
1/2 teaspoon salt
2 cups mild cheddar cheese, grated
sour cream, to use as garnish
6 tomatoes, sliced

Preheat oven to 350°. Slit chilies lengthwise on one side only. Remove seeds and place Monterey Jack slices inside. Divide stuffed chilies among eight greased small baking dishes (custard cup size). In medium size bowl, mix together eggs, milk, flour, and salt, and pour over the chilies.

Sprinkle the top with grated cheddar cheese and bake, uncovered, for 45 minutes.

Garnish each serving with a tablespoon or so of sour cream and a tomato slice. Serves 8.

Good Morning Tarts

pastry for 9-inch pie crust   ground red pepper
4 eggs   lettuce leaves
½ cup whipping cream
2 tablespoons butter, cut into small pieces
¼ pound Swiss cheese, shredded (1 cup)
1 six-ounce package cooked ham, sliced
1 sixteen-ounce can pear halves, drained

Preheat oven to 400°. Prepare pie crust; roll to ¼-inch thick. Using 6-inch round plate as a guide, cut 4 circles from pastry. Set each pastry circle loosely in a 6-ounce custard cup; place some foil in each cup to keep sides from collapsing. Place cups in jellyroll pan; bake 15 minutes, or until pastry is golden brown. Cool pastry in cups for 5 minutes. Remove pastry from cups; discard foil. Turn oven to 350°. In each pastry cup, sprinkle one-quarter of cheese. Break 1 egg into each; top with 1 tablespoon whipping cream; dot with one quarter of butter. Sprinkle each lightly with ground red pepper. Place pastry cups in jellyroll pan. Bake about 15 minutes for soft centered eggs, or until desired doneness. To serve, arrange one egg tartlet, one or two slices ham, one or two pear halves, and a lettuce leaf on each breakfast plate.

Farmer John's Breakfast

¼ cup margarine
¼ cup diced onion
3 medium potatoes,
    cut into cubes
1 twelve-ounce can
    chopped ham, cut
    into cubes

6 eggs
½ teaspoon salt
¼ cup shredded sharp
    cheddar cheese

Using a large skillet, sauté onion and potatoes in hot margarine until potatoes are slightly browned. Cook covered for 15 minutes, or until potatoes are almost tender. Stir in ham cubes. Beat eggs with salt, and pour over potato mixture. Cook over low flame, occasionally slipping spatula underneath potatoes and ham to let uncooked egg flow to bottom. When eggs are set, sprinkle with cheese. Cover skillet a minute or until cheese is melted. Serves 6.

Cheese Grits Souffle

1½ cups quick grits
2 teaspoons salt
6 cups boiling water
1 pound grated cheddar cheese
3 eggs, beaten
dash of Tabasco sauce

1½ sticks butter, melted
1 tablespoon seasoned salt
⅛ teaspoon paprika
1 teaspoon Worcestershire
  sauce

Cook grits and salt in water for 5 minutes. (If regular grits are used, cook 20 minutes.) Mix all ingredients and pour into well-greased 3 quart casserole. May be refrigerated overnight. Bake 1 hour at 350° or 1½ hours at 275°. Serves 8. Variation: Crumble cooked bacon on top before baking.

Croissant Bake

4 croissants, sliced in half
    lengthwise
¼ pound mozzarella
    cheese, sliced
2 cups shredded gruyère
    cheese
½ pound bacon, cooked
    crisp and crumbled
6 eggs

1 cup milk
salt
pepper
freshly ground nutmeg
½ cup parmesan cheese,
    shredded
parsley

Place croissants sliced side up in baking dish. Place the sliced mozzarella evenly over croissants. Sprinkle with gruyère and bacon. Combine eggs, milk; add salt, pepper, and nutmeg to taste. Pour half of the mixture over the cheese and croissant layer. Place tops of the croissants on top and pour the remaining egg mixture over them. Sprinkle with the parmesan cheese. Bake at 350° for 35 to 45 minutes (cover with foil if it begins to brown too much). Garnish with parsley and serve.

This dish can be assembled a day ahead and stored in the refrigerator overnight, unbaked.

You can create your own variations to this entree, by substituting cooked ham, chicken, crab, or shrimp, for the bacon.

41

Southwest Quiche

½ cup milk
¼ cup all-purpose flour
4 large eggs
3 cups shredded sharp cheddar cheese
1½ cups small-curd cottage cheese
½ cups crushed corn chips
1 teaspoon sugar
1 teaspoon baking powder
Salsa

In a large bowl, smoothly stir milk into flour, then add eggs, cheddar cheese, cottage cheese, corn chips, sugar, and baking powder. Beat until well blended.

Pour into a 9 x 13-inch pan or baking dish. Bake, uncovered in a 350° oven until quiche is slightly puffed and appears set firm when the pan is gently shaken (about 40 minutes). Let cool for 10 minutes, then cut into 12 equal rectangles. Transfer to plates using a wide spatula. Add salsa to taste. Makes 12 servings.

Sweet
Somethings

Blueberry Breakfast Pudding

1 large egg
1/3 light or dark
   brown sugar
1 teaspoon ground cinnamon
1 teaspoon grated lemon rind
1/2 cup plain or vanilla
   lowfat yogurt

2 cups fresh or frozen dry
   pack blueberries, sorted
   stemmed
pinch ground nutmeg
6 slices whole wheat bread
1 cup skim milk
1 teaspoon vanilla extract

With a fork, beat eggs and brown sugar together in a large bowl until well blended. Stir in milk, cinnamon, lemon rind, nutmeg, and vanilla. Tear the bread into 1/2-inch pieces and stir into the mixture. Cover and refrigerate 1 hour or overnight. Preheat oven to 375°. Lightly coat an 8x8x2 inch baking pan with cooking spray. Stir the blueberries into the bread mixture and spoon into the pan, spreading the pudding evenly. (You can sprinkle a little sugar mixed with cinnamon over the top if desired). Bake for 40 minutes uncovered, or until firm. Serve warm, topping each portion with 2 tablespoons of yogurt, if desired. Serves 6.

Heavenly Coffee

1 cup instant coffee
1½ cups powdered milk
½ teaspoon nutmeg
2 cups non-dairy creamer
⅔ to ¾ cup sugar (or use
18 packages of sweetener)
2 teaspoons cinnamon
1 to 2 individual packets of
hot chocolate mix

Mix all ingredients thoroughly. Use 2 to 3 teaspoons
per cup of hot water. Smells heavenly and tastes
even better.

45

Wake Up Shakes

Orange Jubilee

8 ounces plain yogurt
2½ cups milk
1 six-ounce can frozen orange
    juice concentrate
1 teaspoon vanilla

Blend all ingredients until smooth.

Tip: If you want to lose weight or just be extra healthy, use nonfat yogurt and lowfat milk.

Banana Smoothie

1 small banana (ripe)
½ cup favorite fruit yogurt
¾ cup milk
¼ cup orange juice

Blend all ingredients until smooth.

Fruitie Tutti

½ cup milk
2 ice cubes
½ cup sliced fruit of
  your choice
½ teaspoon vanilla

Blend all ingredients until smooth, then
taste. If it needs to be sweeter, use 1 to 2
teaspoons sugar.

The cheerful heart has a
continual feast.
—Proverbs

Banana Breakfast Nog

2 ripe bananas
2 cups milk
2 large eggs

2 tablespoons honey
1 teaspoon vanilla

Peel the bananas and cut into chunks. Put the banana chunks, milk, eggs, honey, and vanilla in a blender and cover. Blend ingredients on medium speed until beverage is thick and frothy. Pour into tall glasses and enjoy right away. Makes 2 servings.

My Sister's Fruit Salsa

2 medium Granny Smith apples
1½ cups fresh strawberries
1 kiwi, peeled
1 small orange
2 tablespoons brown sugar
2 tablespoons apple jelly

Peel, core, and chop apples. Hull strawberries and slice. Peel, core, and chop kiwi. Grate 2 tablespoons of orange zest, squeeze rest of orange to equal ¼ cup of juice. Stir all of the above with brown sugar and apple jelly in a bowl.
Terrific on bread and muffins.

49

Healthy Blueberry Treat

1 large egg
⅓ cup light or
  dark brown sugar
1 cup skim milk
1 teaspoon ground cinnamon
1 teaspoon grated lemon rind
pinch ground nutmeg
1 teaspoon vanilla extract
6 slices whole wheat bread
2 cups fresh or frozen dry pack blueberries,
  sorted and stemmed
½ cup plain or vanilla lowfat yogurt

With a fork, beat egg and brown sugar together in a large bowl until well blended. Stir in milk, cinnamon, lemon rind, nutmeg, and vanilla. Tear the bread into ½-inch pieces and stir into the mixture. Cover and refrigerate for 1 hour or overnight. Preheat oven to 375°. Lightly coat an 8x8x2-inch baking pan with cooking spray. Stir the blueberries into the bread mixture and spoon into the pan, spreading the pudding evenly. (You can sprinkle a little sugar mixed with cinnamon over the top if desired.) Bake for 40 minutes uncovered, or until firm. Serve warm, topping each portion with 2 tablespoons of yogurt, if desired. Serves 6.

Stuffed French Toast

4 ounces softened cream cheese
¼ cup ricotta cheese
8 slices sour dough bread, crusts removed
3 tablespoons blueberry or strawberry preserves
10 eggs, beaten
¼ cup heavy whipping cream
1 tablespoon pure vanilla extract
1 to 2 tablespoons butter
Fresh blueberries or strawberries
Pure maple syrup, heated

In a bowl, beat both cheeses until smooth. Divide cheese among four slices of bread. Dot each slice with preserves. Top each with second slice of bread. In a shallow baking dish, beat eggs, cream, and vanilla. Soak the bread in mixture. In a large frying pan, melt the butter, then brown bread until golden (turn only once). Sprinkle with berries and serve with warm syrup. Serves 4.

It's the little things that count ♥

Fabulous Butterhorns

Pastry

½ cup (2 sticks) butter or margarine
(small curd, cream style)
12 ounces cottage cheese
2 cups flour
pinch of salt

Cream together butter and cottage cheese (do not use electric mixer or processor). Add flour and salt. Refrigerate overnight or for 4 hours. Divide dough into 3 parts and cover lightly with flour. Roll out each part into a flat circle and cut into 12 wedges. Roll into butterhorns—start with wide end and roll toward the point. Bake 30 to 40 minutes at 350°. Frost and serve.

Frosting

2 cups powdered sugar
2 tablespoons butter

½ teaspoon vanilla
2 tablespoons milk

Mix ingredients together, adjusting amount of milk to make a frosting that will spread smoothly.

Norwegian Kringler

1 cup (2 sticks) butter or margarine   2 tablespoons water
2 cups flour   3 eggs

Frosting

1½ cups powdered sugar   1 to 2 teaspoons lemon or
2 tablespoons butter, softened   orange juice
                                               1 teaspoon vanilla

Cut ½ cup butter into 1 cup flour. Add 2 tablespoons water
and mix with fork. Spread on ungreased cookie sheets in 2
3 x 12-inch strips.

Bring to a rolling boil 1 cup water and ½ cup butter or margarine. Remove from heat and add 1 cup flour. Stir over heat
until it forms a ball. Beat in 3 eggs, one at a time, until
smooth. Spread over the strips of dough.

Bake at 350° for 15 to 25 minutes, or until golden brown.
Remove from pan to a wire rack.

In a medium bowl, mix together powdered sugar, butter, lemon
or orange juice, and vanilla. Beat until smooth and creamy.
Frost and enjoy.

Just For Kids

Fruit Pudding

1 pound softened cream cheese
¼ pint heavy whipping cream
2 egg yolks
1 cup sugar
canned fruit (any kind),
  drain before using
graham crackers

Blend first four ingredients until smooth.
Refrigerate until firm. Place graham crackers in
square pan. Spoon pudding over crackers and top
with fruit.

Breakfast Blizzard

¼ cup sliced banana
¼ cup pineapple chunks
¼ cup orange sections
2 tablespoons flaked coconut
1 teaspoon chopped pecans
6 ounces custard style banana yogurt

Mix oranges, pineapple, and banana. Mix coconut and pecans. Alternate layers of fruit, yogurt, and coconut mixture into parfait glasses. Serves 2.

Orange Sponge Waffles

4 eggs, separated
⅔ cup sugar
¼ cup milk
2 teaspoons grated orange peel
1 cup all-purpose flour, sifted
½ teaspoon salt
2 tablespoons sugar
lightly sweetened whipped cream

Beat egg yolks and two-thirds cup sugar together, until
thick and pale yellow. Beat in the milk and orange peel.
Sift the flour with the salt. Beat egg whites until soft
peaks form; gradually beat in the 2 tablespoons sugar
until mixture is glossy. Fold egg yolk mixture and flour
mixture into beaten egg whites. Spoon batter into preheated
waffle baker and bake until lightly browned. Makes four
6x10 ½-inch waffles. Serve with lightly sweetened
whipped cream sprinkled with finely grated orange peel.

Cocoa-Nut Muffins

1 package semi-sweet chocolate
1 pound butter
1 package coconut
1 cup nuts
3½ cups sugar
8 eggs
2 cups flour
2 teaspoons vanilla

Mix, pour into greased muffin cups, and bake in
325° oven for 35 minutes. Serves 30.

Baked Bananas

2 eggs, well beaten
4 bananas, peeled and halved lengthwise
⅔ cup chopped almonds
3 tablespoons melted butter or margarine
2 tablespoons sugar
1 tablespoon cinnamon
½ teaspoon ginger

Dip bananas in the beaten eggs, then roll in almonds. Place in buttered baking dish. Pour melted butter over bananas. Mix sugar, cinnamon, and ginger. Sprinkle over bananas. Bake at 350° for 40 minutes.

Peanut Butter Toast

1 cup applesauce
1 teaspoon cinnamon
2 slices of bread
2 tablespoons peanut butter (creamy)

Heat applesauce in microwave for 1 minute.
Add cinnamon, then set aside. Toast bread.
Spread on the peanut butter. Pour applesauce
mixture on top of each piece of toast.
Makes 2 servings.

Index of Recipes

May green be the
grass you walk on,

May blue be the skies
above you.

May pure be the joys
that surround you,

May true be the hearts
that love you.

····OLD IRISH BLESSING····